The Golden Thread

to my father

Pattern &
The Golden Thread

India Russell

images by
Lil Tudor-Craig

Paekakariki Press
2014

This is number **84**
*from an edition
of 350 copies.*

© 2014 India Russell
images © 2014 Lil Tudor-Craig
www.tudor-craig.co.uk

Set in
12pt Garamond

Printed at the
Paekakariki Press, Walthamstow
paekakarikipress.com

ISBN: 978-1-908133-15-1

Contents

SPRING BECOMING SUMMER

The Tryst	3
March 2003	4
What's On?	5
Suburban Garden in April	6
Today the Wind is King	8
Maytime	9
Do not be impatient	10
The Leaf	11

SUMMER BECOMING AUTUMN

The Curve in the Road	15
Wonder	16
The Everlasting Marriage	17
Summer Storm	18
The Voice of Poseidon	20
The Breakthrough or Vision of Arcadia	21
The Handkerchiefs	22
Dandelion Clocks	23
The Faery Howe	24

AUTUMN BECOMING WINTER

Three Poems of Dusk	29
Song for September	30
Morning Walk in an October Garden	31
The Willow's Lament	32
November View from a Window	34
Late November Afternoon	35
The Visitors	36
The Duke's Mistress & The White Horse	38
Margaret's Lament	40

Intimations of Spring

Drifting away from the Grey	45
Paradise Copse	46
Vision in January	47
The Lane to Paradise	48
'And only man is vile'	49
What does it matter?	50
The Fragmenting of the Pattern	52
The Herald of Glory	53
The Pattern of the Day	54
The Seagull Speaks	56

Spring becoming Summer

The Tryst

A chill and rainy dusk in March
Traffic with its terrible sirens
Filtering through the air
While whining aircraft score the innocent heavens.

The blackbirds, though, are singing
As if the world were new and undefiled,
A divine source of jubilation,
While, far off, two lovers' silhouettes
Enhance the darkening sky

Coming together, hesitantly, they seem
To fall upon each others necks,
Retreat a little, then return to their embrace.

The hymning of the birds increases
Night slowly falls
And silently the two crows leave
Their tall and loving tree
And fly majestically towards the welcoming woods
                                      and home.

March 2003

March is an upsetting month
Ill at ease, blustery, quick bursts of temper
And then all smiles, as gradually the urgent force
Of Spring bursts cosy buds, cracks open corms and bulbs
Sends spiralling shoots into the chilly air
While birds sing thinking of the tasks before them.

And in the silly world of humans
Loud mowers make their angry débuts in suburban
                                                     gardens
Trees shudder as the chainsaw's shadow darkens
Patios are polished and toxic killers sprayed
While shops pile up the shoddy paraphernalia of
                                                     Summer
Ready for the ghastly revellers.

And while man threatens this sad, noble planet
With his deadly weapons of destruction
The little blue butterfly gets ready for the Spring

Ready to flit across the shadowy gardens
Like another coloured sun
Ready to rest in jewelled splendour
On a welcoming leaf, new sprung for the occasion,
Ready to fill the eye and heart
With secret messages from another world
Of Truth and Beauty, Love and deep Compassion

Ready to move my sorrowing soul to tears.

What's On?

Tonight, I watched with anxious anticipation
In case, this time, the production engineers
Had got it wrong,
The rising of the full moon.

Telephone turned off, glass of wine to hand
House lights turned down
I awaited the emergence of the
Glowing goddess — her appearance
Heralded by back-lit trees and bushes.

The tension was unbearable.
Would sudden cloud ruin the performance?
Would it really happen?
Could we depend upon her dedication
Her loyalty to this particular venue?
Had she finally tired of
Our sad theatre with its rotting stalls
And Royal Boxes ready to collapse,
Tired of such thin, unappreciative audiences,
                            of genuine response?

    But no! Her aureole rises now above the trees
    And, Yes, she's here
    Glorious and brilliant, flooding this
    Undeserving theatre with her beauty.

Suburban Garden in April

Two pigeons lift into the air
And slide, skidding down the wind
And, like young mountain streams,
High aspens murmur tricklingly.

Apple blossoms shower confetti blessings
On a robin and his bride
Bouncing beneath beneficent boughs.

(How lovely to have such a wedding
And such witnesses.)

Squirrels, furry Æoluses
Gust through the flowing trees
And a flight of unknown birds
Swishes above my head like
Ballgowns sweeping down a noble staircase.

(If only I lived in that house
And wore such a gown.)

The old yew trees are lit up suddenly by a blue flower
Darting round their dusky, kindly forms.
Is it the same butterfly, I wonder, that flitted about
The garden, yesterday?

Miraculous hover-flies hover
Pigeons continue to skim, lift, drop and skim again
Bees hum and work too hard, as
Ants seriously pursue their tasks.

The robins sing now, while
Magpies bustle in the hazel tree
And busy bluetits hop in the japonica.

Squirrels, still defying gravity, curvet,
Echoing the little butterfly
Tracing a sky-trail through the garden
While a blackbird alights, singing,
In the holy apple tree.

> Only I am out of place here,
> Only I wish to be somewhere and somebody else
> Only I do not add to the scene
> But burden it.

> Only I am idle and tuneless
> In this Paradise Garden.

Today the Wind is King
poem for the end of April

Today the wind is king.
Trees bend to his command,
Dust, litter, people, cats
Accommodate themselves to his cold gusts
And windows shiver.

Only the birds make fun of his proud sway
Gay, dancing, flying on his back then dropping
Turning, whirling, drifting, soaring up towards infinity
Then resting for a moment, statuesque-like forms,
Motionless, upon the wild and tossing air
While I, indoors, a flightless human, follow their wide
                              pattern.

Three crows, I think, too far too see,
Whirl round and round, now almost touching,
                              dropping
Now falling far apart, then back together
Wheeling upwards, boundless, beyond sight,
Laughing at the wind

Who now moans sadly round the house's stolid walls
While I return to my small, boundaried world
                    anchored by dull gravity.

Maytime

The days are long enough to live and die in.
Old age, maturity and youth all flicking
Through the hours, resting a moment
And then passing with the ticking seconds
While the Sun moves through his ancient path
And mayflies die upon his setting.

One day is long enough to feel the weal and woe of life,
Trees burgeoning into unbelievable beauty
The blackbird hymning his too poignant

                                        song of praise

Man crashing through their
Web of magic, like Polyphemus mad with

                                        blinding pain

While tears
        spring from one's depths
                of helplessness and love
                        and heartbreaking compassion.

Do not be impatient

Do not be impatient
                    with the tree and bee
For their time is not your Time.
Do not hurry the trapped insect from
The window-sill, allow him space and
Freedom to escape into the welcoming air
Wishing him well upon his lovely flight.

Do not lop, thoughtlessly, limbs from
The singing tree — first stand in awe
Before this God, then offer your praise and
                              put away the saw;
And go and re-read *Mountain Lion*.

Their time is not your Time
             neither the lion's nor the bee's
For they have no time — but live in pure
Eternity, shedding continually its
Celestial Light upon this sorry Earth.

Time is a man-made inconvenience
And Impatience its tedious daughter.
Rise beyond their imprisoning grasp
And catch the flakes
Of glimpsed Eternity in Nature's song and all her
                              innocent progeny's
                                  wondrous beauty

But do not be impatient.

The Leaf

Sitting in the spoon-back chair
Whose lines and mellow craftmanship
Are always pleasing,
Transported dreamily back to childhood
By the summoning scent of lilac
I gazed upon a leaf, back-lit
By the table lamp

And suddenly, I awakened into yet another
World of singing and harmonious wonder,
For here were forking paths, strange lights,
Beautiful designs,
A speaking pattern beyond thought and craft,
A world of mystery
Beyond our human compass

And returning to the confines of the present room,
I wondered yet again how man
Could think himself the measure of all things
In the pure light of one single leaf of lilac.

Summer becoming Autumn

The Curve in the Road

I see it now
The curve in the road where we had stopped,
The quiet inn and swooping swallows,
The view of distant hills

It seemed as though we had stepped out
Beyond the clamour of the daily world
Into a fairy tale,
We'll come back, we said,
Stay at the inn and find
Ourselves again

We never did return.

Wonder

Felix is dreaming of the willow tree.
Last evening, as the wind arose,
He lay beneath its streaming branches
Staring up into its greeny vaults

And as the wind caught one and then another
Weeping strand, he played with it as with
                                        a friend,
His feline eyes the colour of the leaves,
His flowing grace an echo of the tree's.

And I, a poor observer of this mystery,
Stand yet again, unlike the master cat,
A novice on the threshold of philosophy
Which, for us both, begins with wonder.

The Everlasting Marriage

Over the timeless sea the gulls sail
While babies and old people are wheeled along its edge
And innocent children try to catch its secret
                                  in a pail.

Last night the moon rose, heavy, orange-red
Departing slowly from its singing depths
Where lusty mermen and wild mermaids murmur
                                  on its bed.

And once again the sun shines, hot and
Mesmeritic, drawing man down into the
Waves' embrace, a sudden mystic union of the
                                  sea and land

Which, perhaps, is why D.S. has etched
A voluptuous, giant heart, bearing the
Legend, I ♥ JOE LUCKERETT 4 EVER
                                  in the sand

Where even now the worms are making little
Mountains and the encroaching sea is shaping her
                                  sworn love
Into another form, a sea-change, an everlasting
Marriage of the eternal and the now of
Joe Luckerett and D. S., this day's and forever's
                                  wondering lovers.

Summer Storm

The houses and buildings were just dead ghosts
Standing where they'd been planted, ugly or mellow,
But soon to crumble into nothingness and
Even now turned to mere shadows by the powerful rain.

But the trees with their sheltered creatures, the trees
Grew mightily, moved over the land like the gods
They had always been, stretching their magnificent limbs
To the sky where Zeus in his element strode angrily
Hurling his lightning spears over the ungrateful
Mortals now inhabiting his holy Earth.

Too long they had forgotten the Gods, these men,
Too long been slaves to their time-bound greed
Too long had thought themselves to be gods
And he was angry, angry.

The nymphs had been driven from the
Glades, his trees killed and mutilated,
The earth and her divine progeny poisoned and wasted;
And so, leaving Olympus, Zeus turned his wrath upon
                                      mortals.

And some, it is true, were afeared, some thought
The end of the world was in sight and some resolved
To be better, to live more in harmony with Nature
To appreciate the trees and the air and the divine
Singing of birds. Oh, yes, in fear of their lives and their
Homes, these thoughts came to many.

And then the storm passed. The thunder of rain
And shiver of lightning a mere fading memory, the world
Carried on as before
              but Zeus, angry Zeus, called
A council of Gods and is planning, even now,
                              his next move.

The Voice of Poseidon

Looking from my hotel window
I saw an overpowering sculptured sea of
Cavernous waves and rearing, fearsome crags,
Smooth massive curves and angles,
As though hewn by some great artist from
Another world, who understood
                the mysteries of the living rock.

I could not turn away, too terrifying was the sight
And so I tried to readjust my vision — and suddenly
Far out, there moved at looming speed
High white-fringed, green-glass walls
Whose supernatural power reduced to nothing
The little world behind me.

I closed my eyes, bereft of flight,
                              and waited

Time stopped

And as its petty measure
Began to draw me back into its hold,
I saw a bright green, level sea
Sparkling as though it were some gentle greensward
Inviting leisurely strolls and comforting discussion.

I turned to my companion,
But saw he had seen nothing.
The strange vision had been for me alone
        to carry with me through the common day.

The Breakthrough or Vision of Arcadia

In the bank on a tearing suburban high street
Where litter and loud advertising
                             hold their own
The man before me in the queue,
Irregularly dressed, it's true,
No dull and slouching uniform
But a style that showed some
Individuality, broke
From this unromantic Century
And, proffering his cheque book,
Addressed the girl behind
The counter. 'Hallo, rosy cheeks,'
He said, in pleasant tones of long ago

                       and suddenly

Birds sang,
       uncaring Time stopped wonderingly and
Gazed anew upon the lovely
Meadows flushing in the sun,
The glinting river,
The gentle breezes as they moved amongst the
Welcoming trees beneath whose bowering branches
Love-lorn shepherds
Sang their melodious songs to blushing maidens

While all the pure, enchanting intricacies
Of simple Nature
            arose
                      and held the moment in eternity

The Handkerchiefs

As a little girl, I believed it,
Walked along the hollyhock-edged path
In crinoline and bonnet,
Birds floating in an azure sky,
The little green gate leading to a world
Where the embroidery did not go;

But my imagination did as, gazing on the
Handkerchiefs in their cardboard box,
I inhabited that magic garden,
And, hollyhock-high,
Surrounded by its secret airs,
I wandered in a paradise.

And suddenly, today,
The glimpse of home returns,
The breath of flowers is borne upon the air
The green beyond is vibrant;
And though the lace is torn now, the
Lawn delicate with age, I know the garden
Is not mere embroidery.

Dandelion Clocks

We used to tell the time
By blowing dandelion seeds
And with the glow of buttercups
Tell whether we liked butter,
Ease nettle burns with dock leaves
And count petals to find who were
Our true loves

But then came man's estate
And the reasonable approach

But no avail
I still dismiss his silly time
                    with dandelions.

The Faery Howe

You *could* say it was the slanting sunlight
On that autumnal August evening
That lit the tree so strangely;

You could say, that as I put my pen down
And looked up from my garden seat
Towards the glowing grassy bank,
It was imagination that made me see
The leaning gnarled old apple tree
Transformed into a Green Man,
Head crowned with fecund branches,
Heaving himself with powerful shoulders from
The sheltering Earth, while birds listened and
                                        trees watched.

You could deny the vision;
But what of Sidhe and the Sylvan Elves?
Or Reverend Kirk of Aberfoyle in Scotland,
His strange account of life beneath The Mound
— a Faery Howe close to his church,
And his friendship with its dwellers whose
Stories he then heard of cruel persecutions by
Recent predatory Man, who drove them from the
                                      surface of the Earth?

Or you could agree with Kirk's belief in
Fellow creatures in the invisible world who, naturally
At home with birds and animals and all Nature,
Correspond as well with us, who are, in fact, a part of Life,
That wondrous and far greater part that occasionally
                                      one glimpses.

      All views depend upon the viewer.
      The uniform hunched humans, policed
      By deadening screens, by some would
      Seem a strange phenomenon, a frightening
                                        distortion.

And what of numerous accounts
From Ireland, Wales or Norway of
The Elemental Beings, Faeries and
The Commonwealth of Elves?

Yes, you could say it was a trick of light
That August evening in the magical garden
But, also, you could say the grassy bank
For centuries had been a Faery Howe
From which I saw an Elemental Being emerging
From The Lands Beneath — a messenger
With wise and timely greetings from
                              the mysterious Faeries.

Autumn becoming Winter

Three Poems of Dusk

1

Tall yellow daisies
Gleam in the darkening garden
Beacons in a strange sea.

2

A solitary bat's fast
Curvetting shadow in the dusk.
Is he lonely too?

3

Night falls. Two crows skim
Towards the welcoming tree
Sleepy leaves murmur.

Song for September

And now the robin sings about the house
Sad songs of wasted summers.
His melancholy notes
Are like a wild prayer of forgiveness
For gross man's stupid sins —
His noisy concentration on himself, his inability
To see the miracle of butterfly or bee
The double-winged dragonfly whirring overhead
The crows at evening skidding down the sky
Towards the outstretched, welcoming tree
The Sun's long, warm embrace and
        Æther's gentleness.

But now long healing rain falls gently in the gardens
Which echoed with the strident shouts of humans
  and the holy robin sings to my sad soul
    mourning yet another, unpraised Summer.

Morning Walk in an October Garden

Yes, the web's still there strung between known leaves
The silent spider poisedly centred in his creation;
The robin is still there, hidden, singing quietly in the bushes
Now surprising me by landing like a parachutist
Near my feet.

The dew is there sparkling on each blade of grass
And the yellowing leaf still dangles
On an unseen thread, twirling in an unfelt breeze.

The crows still hold their parliament
And magpies argue with the jays
While, silently, the magnificent crane
Glides, like a dream of Leonardo's, overhead.

Yes, nothing's changed, it seems, but
                            the invisible, inexorable hand of Time.

The Willow's Lament

It would have been better
To have cut me to the quick
And let me die.
That would have been a partial release
A transformation.

But to mutilate me, to climb into
My loving limbs and bloodily hack my
Flowing branches from me,
To strip me to the bone and leave me
Naked to the Winter's blast
And the terrible prospect of a deformed life,
That was a cruel act that
Only man can execute.

The resounding shock still
Echoing through the vaults of heaven,
I know the trusting creatures that I housed
Are wondering why their home has gone
As, restlessly, the wind sighs for
The lyre of my weeping tresses
While, beyond help and motionless, I stand here,
A rhythmless, mute giant
Amongst the sad and moving world of innocent Nature.

> And I, inside my silly flimsy house,
> Feel his lamentations in my soul
> And mourn with him
> The great malignèd God
> With whom I've shared my life
> These few and fleeting years

And, once again, regret I am a member of
The race of man
For whom, as with so many of Nature's gifts,
The willow's great and mystic majesty
Was unwanted
A magnificence beyond his comprehension
And, tragically,
               beyond the grace of his compassion.

November View from a Window

Iridescent against the sun-shot darkening sky
A company of seagulls sparkles by
And trees, autumnal in this dallying warmth,
Stand gold and green, still leafy shelters
For the magpie, wren and dove.

But soon, they know, their glory will be stripped
By winds and biting cold, revealing their old
Firm structures, wonderful branching shapes
Of Winter, still offering peace and rest to
Birds and squirrels, a home between the sky and earth.

Let's light the fire and talk of oft-told family tales,
Draw the curtains on our little world, while
Outside, and far beyond our knowing, the trees
Relate their history to the surrounding gods.

Late November Afternoon

So close to another dimension,
So thinly divided
     and as dusk
Sifts through the Autumn air
And trees stretch out their welcoming
Silhouettes, my soul grows luminous
With the sky, begins to fly
       so close to home it hurts

      and then it's dark

And yet another chance of entering Reality
        is lost,
Time reasserts its sway and carelessly
Continues on its bound and dreary way.

The Visitors

And so they hovered lovingly
About the place that had been theirs,
A joyous home of laughter, fun and
Stories of old times,
Discussions of the meaning of existence
                                  around the comforting fire,
The strangeness of this human race,
The haphazard nature of creation.

They smiled and entered in —
The quest for a solution to the
Mystery of being had been the subject
For generation upon generation,
Only the variants gave colour to the
                                  unsolved argument.

Why, then, were they drawn to this
Particular house, and this particular
Discussion? They had, of course,
Lived here, held similar questing converse
Within its mellow walls
But they knew it was not that which
Drew them from their sphere.

Was it because, this time,
The timeless glimpse of unity,
The sudden understanding of the
Harmony of matter — the star,
The stone, the butterfly and mole,
The dreaming nights of vision,
Was now reality, not just conjecture following
                                  fleeting revelation;

Had they been called
To finally assist
In the conversion of the ideal to the real?

The air changed, growing chill,
The conversation flagged — but as it did
The fire and candles, erstwhile mimics
Of past gas-lit shadowy charm, flared high and bright
Casting strange radiance upon the lovely room

And in that moment
The guests awoke and, looking out of different eyes,
Beheld a world of light and beauty
                            and of blinding truth.

The Duke's Mistress & The White Horse

to Mark

Rising with Venus on the waves of love
Borne upon the moving powers of Nature,
She becomes, in his embrace, the Goddess.
No longer dull-visaged, poor of stature, weak,
The butt of serving maids and gossips,
The transformation in that four-poster bed
                                     is consummate
She is the Duke's belovèd goddess,
                                     as ravishing as Helen.

And so, year after year, century after century,
The White Horse beckons,
The patient ostler waiting at his colour-paned window
Looking out onto the cobbled entrance to the stables,
The child playing without noise,
Running heedlessly amongst the servants' legs,
And then, suddenly, the stillness,
The log fires flickering low,
The surrounding air fast chilling
As The White Horse welcomes, once again,
Her silent entrance to the inn.

> Many times they have been seen by guests
> Some are frightened but
> Chamber maids are unperturbed

And still she waits, The Duke's Mistress,
Waits for the rumbling clatter of the ducal carriage
Waits for his regal tread upon the stair and then,
More urgently, along the passage to their chamber,
Waits for the turning handle
The rush of ardent warmth
The final melting fire of passion.

But, always now, he is detained,
Affairs of State, perhaps, or the Duchess and
Her demanding children?
Yet confident that The White Horse, with its
Canny eye, will draw him back — she waits

Waits, through all the flying years,
While below, the ostler and the child wait with her,
Waits, still waits, for her belovèd Duke
Confident in the knowledge that his consuming love
                              will be for ever.

Margaret's Lament

But I'm still your loving mermaid and
I hear the children calling
And I mourn, so mourn my terrible mistake

> When I broke the deep enchantment
> As the bells came sounding softly
> And drew me up into the banishing, cold air.
>
> When they came like grim, stern warders
> And took me from your palace,
> From your everlasting kingdom,
> From your pearl and amber chambers
> Where, at last, within your arms
>   I had found peace
>
> Where, transformed into myself now, I felt
> The universal rhythms, the flow of all the oceans
> Heard the amorous sailing whales and the
>   soothing sound of fishes
> As they listened to the answering stars.
>
> In those glinting lovely caverns
> Midst the light and sounding rushes
> In the hushing flowing waters
> I, like Ellida, had found my element;
> And, oh, I loved you, oh,
>   I loved you so

I never told you how it happened
In the fractured world above you
How I found myself within your shining realm;
As, in one flash of vision,
Like the playing cards of Alice,
I saw, in all its bombast, Time collapse.
And in that timeless moment
I suddenly came upon you and we loved
                        and lived as in a dream

But then the iron bell
With its rhythmless persuasion
Chained me back into the
                        time-bound careless world
I said I would not stay long
Would be back upon the instant
Would soon again be free, within your arms

But that was long ago now
And the nights are long and dreary,
And the iron bonds are heavy
As they tie me to the coldly glaring day

The gentle rain is sighing
And the winds moan, oh, so loudly

    But I'm still your loving mermaid and
    I hear the children calling
    And I mourn, so mourn
                        my terrible return.

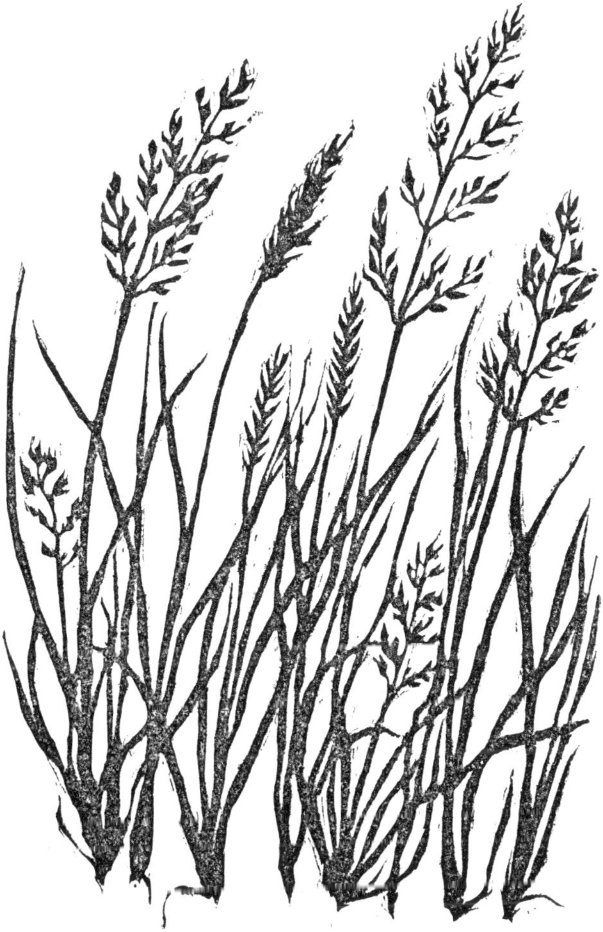

Intimations of Spring

Drifting away from the Grey

Trees tower and are absorbed
Into the whiteness of the Winter skies
And little birds become them.

Fine rain slowly mists the human grey
And through its slanting gifts
Another world is seen, where Gods
Magnificently move in other, nobler rhythms
And the curves and patterns
Etched upon the watery and translucent air
By squirrels, birds and dark embracing branches
Reveal a place of strange enchantment,
Ancient and at one and wholly

And so movingly familiar that it
Seems if only one could drift
Into its wondrous midst
Then one would finally be at home and
                      know the meaning of to be.

Paradise Copse

The year's last day!
Tree, earth and bush accept the rain's caress
And wait expectantly.

Crows, strangely large,
Stand still and black on solemn oaks and
From a distant house
Faint smoke winds gently upwards to the sky.

Within the copse
Two squirrels search for nuts hid long ago
And play a game of chase among the leaves.

Even a little flower is blooming in the hedge,
All silently and still

And deer, as innocent as day
Leap over ditches,
Light as air.

The little goldcrest hops,
A gleam of joy among the trees,
From branch to branch
And blackbirds scold my presence from a
Further bush

The squirrels argue now,
And in the treetops
Rasp their anger in a squawky voice.

Then all is still,
Save for the gentle
Falling of the rain
On this eternal song.

Vision in January

I love the colour of days
                      that is no colour;
Rain on the wind and a parliament of trees,
Silhouettes of sailing birds.

No brightness to strike the eye,
No lights to dazzle, no imposing forms
In this now muted place
But an enchanting many-dimensional sketch
                    of wondrous pattern
Etched with slanting rain

A secret, magic world that leads the
Enlivened soul on
                    to vistas of eternity.

The Lane to Paradise

Sometimes, dwelling in our quiet
Companionship, my spirit wandering
Through a maze of memories and dreams,
Dear Felix suddenly purrs so loudly,
Turning round to look into my eyes,
It seems as though he's there
Within my musing.

It happened again today when,
Far away in Devon,
In the lane to *Paradise* from *Whidown*
I gradually found his purring presence with me
There, beneath the rain-dark shining trees,
Shafts of sudden sunlight
Lighting up his fur, the raindrops and the stream,
Gilding the lilting deer and chasing squirrels
With magic and with mystery.

And I wondered if my sage companion,
Who never in reality knew *Whidown*,
Had seen the beauty of my vision,
And was pleased to be there, with me,
Walking along the lane to *Paradise*.

'And only man is vile'
on men shooting in woods near Paradise

Sigh, trees, sigh!
Man is a sorry fool.
All through this majesty of woods
He insignificantly struts
And shoots at what he
Does not understand.

Fly, birds, fly!
And mock this earth-bound
Creature with your flight

Rage, trees, rage.

What does it matter?

i.m. Sir Richard Acland who, as a member of J. B. Priestley's Common Wealth Party, gave his 19,000 acre estate to the National Trust, apart from the land on which was situated our family home of Whidown

'It doesn't matter about bloody central heating!
The planet, now, is dying
The human race is hurtling to destruction!'

We were at home at *Whidown*, in
That lovely room looking towards
The tors of Dartmoor, while from the southward
Windows were glimpsed the Devon cliffs.

We'd been listening to Schubert, my brother played it well;
Dinner had passed, an unremembered fare,
And now we all were round the blazing fire,
Bound together with such familiar skeins,
They seemed to link us to
Those great spirits we talked about;

And I felt strongly that this was how
We'd always be
Questing through the mystery of life,
I always could come back and sound
My findings against theirs

Then, suddenly, the circle broke —
They were all gone,
My brother, father and my mother,
The physics and the music,
The literature and insights
                              and the laughter

And as I dwell upon my present isolation in
This darkening world that
Priestley and Acland tried to lighten,
My father's words ring through me

    And I remember *Whidown*,
    That home of idealistic hope,
    Which, ironically enough, did not have central heating,
    But did embrace our spirits and our wonderful
                                              discussions
    That led us on towards the warm
                                and everlasting light.

The Fragmenting of the Pattern

It is the fragmenting of the Pattern and the Rhythm
That causes stress.

All around is pattern and design —
A little raindrop and a sweeping shower
Are all melodiously divine.

The miraculous shapes of trees
Etched against a watercolour sky,
The keeling seagulls leaning on the wind,
Two wood pigeons dancing in a loving circle
                            at the touch of Spring —
All proclaim the patterned beauty of Creation

All but man, whose Greed and
Jealousy of what he does not understand
Has closed his inner eye
And left him rebellious, a blind, destructive
                            alien in Paradise.

The Herald of Glory

The snow was not long gone
The rain persistent
The day drew to its damp dark February end
When suddenly I heard the sound
Of glory — a blackbird singing
With such heavenly tones, I felt
Embarrassed to be listening

Too much a novice for such revelation
Too undeserving in this world of traffic and
Closed doors, despair and resignation,
Too unprepared
                          but still he sang,
With tones so pure and innocent
It seemed as though the world were new created
And he its joyful messenger

                        and still I hear him
Drawing me into another sphere of being
And give thanks for those
Spontaneous intimations of a world
                        so often sensed in dreams
And sometimes
           suddenly found
                     in waking life.

The Pattern of the Day

poem on my Birthday

No, I'll not go out today
                         until this evening when we'll dine
                                amongst the throng
           talking of this and that and drinking wine;
I'll stay and merge into the pattern of the day
Heralded by the crows' majestic voices
As they sail between the distant stand of pines and
Magnificent, surrounding trees
And, closer, the homely robin's plaintive song
So out of keeping with his bouncing, friendly manners.

I expect the magpies will look in
Flashing their spectacular black and white amongst
The branches, whose delicate etching now is
Blurred with pulsing thoughts of Spring,
While pigeons coo their unbelievably
Romantic songs of Love.

Too early for the imitative, familiar starlings
But I'll think of them
And of my parents, grandparents and brother;
We'll have a Birthday Party of the Spirit
And I'll thank them for the wondrous gifts
They gave me and still give;
And I'll give thanks for the creator or the
Driving force behind all this
                         all this

      How strange
            how strange
                  this life
                       these deaths
  How beautiful the innocent world of nature

No, I'll not go out today into the throng
But stay
    and merge into the pattern of the day.

The Seagull Speaks

It is raining still
And in the Marine Gardens
I am the only visitor to gaze
Into the plate-glass cage
Where human creatures are being fed.

Cackling together or silently alone
They crouch there, motionless,
And, moved, I cannot look away,
Then, suddenly, I see her — she
Who twice has risen with us, up
Into the sea-blue limits of the sky

And silently I fly and stand upon
Another stack of chairs close to her,
The glass our only barrier.
Her power seems trapped
Weighed down by fear;

'At your mother's funeral you
Flew with us! Remember!'
She stirs and hears me;
'Remember your dream!
Up from primæval slime, you crawled upon the earth
And then, from metamorphosis to metamorphosis,
Higher and higher you rose, until
You were transformed into a heavy-bodied moth
Whose fragile wings grew stronger, stretching out
In powerful rhythm, until, with lightened soul
You were a seagull

And then you flew beyond the sheltering tree
Up into freedom and
                      the infinity of Truth!'

She hears me and remembers;
Though fearful still, she will
Return into her natural realm,
And so I fly away into the rain-washed loving air, trailing
                 the golden thread of recognition.